searching for a pulse

searching for a pulse

poems

Nazifa Islam

Whitepoint Press
San Pedro, California

A Whitepoint Press First Edition 2013

Cover design and illustration by Sarah LaVoie

ISBN-13: 9780615770994
ISBN-10: 0615770991

Library of Congress Control Number: 2013933141

Published by Whitepoint Press
www.whitepointpress.com

for every Sylvia

Contents

32   it has red leaves

33   she won't take 300 mg of lithium

34   treasure hunting

35   she'd bought him a diamond tie

36   always before the alarm goes off

37   everyone has their dreams

38   44 cents

39   a cleaver with a bone handle

40   she's lacking in sentiment

41   she swallowed the fork as well

42   the voice of reason

43   not a drop of blood was spilled

44   he wanted nothing sparkling

45   no forecast of rain

46   but she's not colorblind

47   she wore a red dress

48   it might even be true

49   she wore the diamond tie

50   the room is paneled in black and white tile

he had a peg leg too

She married a man with one glass eye
and divorced him the next day but he
still got his green card. She weeps now
while sitting in front of her television
watching Wheel of Fortune every night.
You haven't met her yet, but her name is Rosemary.

the lighter was green

There is a burn mark
on Rosemary's left wrist
and a lighter in Finn's
jacket pocket. No one
has put two and two
together. They weren't
meant to. Rosemary's
not going to say a word
to anyone which is what
Finn wants even if he
is choked up with guilt –
it wasn't his idea.
Rosemary knows this
it's what has bought
her silence.

now maybe you'll understand

Rosemary broke into two pieces
at seventeen, though nobody really
noticed. Her halves lay in the sand
and grit and mud, soaking up so
much she never wanted to know
before she went and taped herself
back together. Sodden, she couldn't
get the tape to really stick and so it
was only a matter of time before
she became someone she didn't like.
She grew fond of knives and blue
pills and boys with brown beards
who smiled crooked moonshadow
smiles at her when they were
certain she was looking right at
them. She met Finn at twenty and
didn't try to die until almost
twenty-one. He didn't know she
was cracked in all the wrong ways
but she felt guilty enough that she
enlightened him as soon as her lips
had stopped bleeding.

he wasn't trying to lie

Rosemary is thinking about the day
the world ended – when everything
turned a pale shade of blue and the
earth flipped itself inside out on a
dare. She remembers it like it was
yesterday – she's not certain it wasn't
yesterday. But when she asks Finn
to tell her the truth about whether or
not her hair looked black under blue
light all he'll say is he's never seen
her before in his life.

it was lemonade-colored ash

Finn will grow to hate
Rosemary when enough
time has passed to cloud
his judgment. He'll blame
her for the color of his beard
and he won't be wrong to
hate her even if his beard
does look better cerulean.
Alice is different. Alice
burned Rosemary's picture
last week on Tuesday before
vacuuming up the small
pile of time immemorial.
They only speak when
people are staring now.

she's never owned a cat

If you asked her, she would say
she hasn't slept in twenty-three
days. Rosemary lies all the time.
She's good at it and she knows
that she is good at it. Not anyone
else does. Not Finn, not Alice, not
Ivan who's new. She lies when
not speaking, she lies when not
eating. She's not really a redhead.
She lied to the world and now it
can't help but stare at her in shock.
No one lies to the world.

he was naked too

They were in bed together
when Rosemary said *I love
you*. They'd only known each
other five weeks. Rosemary
wasn't wearing red like she'd
been planning – she wasn't
wearing anything at all. Before
Finn could sneer or smile or
laugh she made certain to add
*don't worry, I wouldn't say it if
it was true*.

her oven was electric

The first time it happened
was on May 15th. It was
snowing outside. Rosemary
wasn't cold though and she
wanted very much to be
numb. She swallowed three
blocks of ice but when that
did nothing she chased the
ice with eighty blue pills.
She started shivering ten
minutes later and fell asleep
content. Finn found her
after she'd stopped breathing
and Alice found Finn sobbing.
She walked away when
Rosemary began to vomit.
Pale green and on oxygen,
she turned twenty-one five
days later. Rosemary has
tried to die eight times and
only succeeded twice.

her thoughts were with the green lighter

Rosemary once thought of dousing
herself in kerosene and lighting
her body and soul aflame. She
thought it would be a spectacle
of an ending as well as a valiant
precursor for Hell itself. But she'd
once before burned herself lighting
Alice's birthday candles and the
sharp stabbing pain – so different
from the dull aching satisfaction
of a razor blade – made her wary
when what she needed was reckless
abandon. Rosemary stares into
mirrors now whenever she can't
help it and the sight of her pale face
and grey eyes instead of a horrible
mask of red scales never fails
to remind her of one simple fact:
what a damned coward you are.

she's never tried heroin

Rosemary wanted to see herself
clearly so she borrowed Alice's
copy of *Requiem for a Dream* and
watched it over and over and
over again. The likeness was
uncanny and the shame which
stole over her at seeing what she
was meant to despise made her
reach for the pill bottle like
withdrawal never had – and she
had caved every time the hot
flashes and shaking and vomiting
had become too much. It was
while weeping that she realized
she truly was pathetic. This
became Rosemary's sixth bid for
freedom but it was not one of
her successes.

he always wears a fedora

Ivan is tall in a way people are never
tall. Rosemary appreciates this. It
tells her she's right in guessing he's
not actually there even if he is always
there – a massive presence standing
within six feet of her person. Ivan
is made of the same foreign substance
dreams are drawn from so when
he vanished one Tuesday morning
Rosemary panicked; she knew how
hard it would be to find and cling to
such vapor. But she still had to try
as without him she felt too small to
even attempt to grasp at loneliness –
and that was a fate impossible to
bear. It took Rosemary four hours
to find him and for the first time in
all their time together she was so
overwhelmed with joy that without
thinking about it she kissed him.

they leave scars

Thoughts are heavy. That was Alice's
excuse to return all of Rosemary's
secrets. Rosemary understood – the
burden had been too much for her
as well. This logic didn't keep her from
crying though. She threw out half her
weighty pile and swallowed another
quarter before shoveling the remaining
thoughts into Finn's arms and asking
him to be careful. He did his very best
but in the end his arms grew tired.
Rosemary has nothing left to hold
or give away now.

her own valiant effort succeeded

She asked no one to take care of
her but they all tried anyway and
were unjustly angry when their
valiant efforts went unrewarded.
She remained Rosemary despite
all the prodding – very slightly
mad and not at all beautiful. Alice
couldn't change any of this and
she tried harder than anyone
before had dared. Finn couldn't
manage anything either. In the
beginning, he actually held to the
insane notion that there was
nothing wrong with Rosemary.
Three months was all it took to
choke that possibility to death but
all the same he found he couldn't
bear to consider leaving her.

the water was warm

Janet held Rosemary
under the water long
after she'd finally
drowned. An hour
before there had been
thrashing as too much
saltwater burned at
Rosemary's lungs and
she tried to scream at
the rippling mass of
blonde hair all of eight
inches above her. This
would be counted
Rosemary's second
success if it wasn't
murder instead of
suicide. Janet laughed
until blood gurgled up
from her lips when
Rosemary woke up
and finding herself
alive once again
started bawling.

he was taught truths

He told Rosemary
she was pretty when
she isn't for a very
long time. Finn isn't
particularly kind he
just actually believed
she was beautiful.
Rosemary used to
roll her eyes at him
but she was secretly
pleased all the same.
He stopped saying
it though after Janet
leaned over one
morning to whisper
I used to think she was
beautiful too but I've
learned better now.

she uses a ballpoint pen

When Rosemary is bored or thinking
about wanting to die, she will trace
her veins in blue ink. She explained
to Alice that it's just to make them
more lifelike. She only traces the veins
in her wrists and over time that has
become a challenge as she has so
many scars cloaking them and making
it difficult to once again slice them
open. It really was so easy the first
time, when she used her father's letter
opener to try and sever her hand
from her wrist. The hand refused
to fall off but when she saw a fountain
of blood pooling onto the carpet
she was satisfied all the same.

she doesn't call herself an insomniac

Three in the morning bodes well
for no one. Rosemary never sleeps
before four but she can bear the
night just fine until three o' clock
when anxiety is unchained and
given leave to seize her around
the throat so long as it never
draws blood. She is forced to
learn lessons then that she was
able to shun in daylight and forget
in the quiet of normal waking hour
so that by half past three she's
touched by madness and spends
the long seconds murmuring over
and over and over again to herself
*Didn't you know this story was
going to have an ending?*

withdrawal is coming

Rosemary's hands are shaking.
She has beautiful eyes but if you
saw how her hands are shaking
you wouldn't be envious. She
hasn't slept in days. That's what
she told Alice and for once it's
almost true. She's had dreams
that are more than dreams for
over a week now and she's
swallowed pill after small blue
pill for over a week now – first
to try and sleep and then to try
and forget she's not sleeping.
Nothing has worked as it was
intended though and so her
hands are now shaking. Even if
she could pry the top off the pill
bottle she knows that it's empty
and that scares her more than
the fact that her fucking hands
won't stop shaking.

someone burned cigarettes

Rosemary wasn't looking
for ash to swallow but she
found a pile anyway. Her
mouth is coated in grey
now and she's choking as
she writhes on the floor.
Finn would help her if he
was there but this time
around he isn't. Alice is
frozen in horror and Janet
is cackling in her corner.
Alice doesn't like Janet and
Janet doesn't like anyone
but in the end they'll team
together to save Rosemary.
Someone always saves
Rosemary. She wants to hate
them for that but somehow
she can't quite manage.

lavender-scented stationery

The fourth time Rosemary
tried to die she decided to
do the thing properly. She
wrote goodbye letters to
everyone she loved and
mailed them before slitting
her wrists. As Rosemary
lay in her hospital bed,
restrained and under
sedation, both Alice and
Finn stopped by to burn
their letters in front of her.
They'd decided *I love you –
but not quite enough* was far
from being adequate. To
this day, Janet sulks about
not getting a letter.

the repetition drove her mad

Selfish creature. Ivan never says
anything but those two words.
He follows Rosemary around all
day and hisses bitingly *Selfish
creature* under his breath. She
can't make him stop though
she's tried – he refuses to bleed
and she's finally convinced he's
not real. *Selfish creature.* Hearing
it one too many times, Rosemary
began to believe he was right
and resolved to make amends.
She bought both Alice and Janet
chocolate and decided to say
goodbye to Finn.

it has red leaves

She's been growing fear
on the inside of her jacket
pocket for many years
now. She meant to give
it away to all the people
who asked her for advice
but as no one came to her
for the very longest time
she decided to torture
Rosemary instead. Janet
gave her fear disguised
as pressed flowers for her
twentieth birthday and
so infected Rosemary for
life. She told Rosemary
what she'd done two
years later and instead of
stabbing her in the neck
Rosemary thanked her
kindly before going off
to moan alone.

she won't take 300 mg of lithium

Sometimes, though not very
often, Rosemary worries about
what people think of her. She
worries about Finn, and she
worries about Alice, she even
worries about Ivan though he's
made of fiction and dreams
but she never bothers to worry
about Janet. Somehow Rosemary
doesn't give a damn if Janet
thinks she's nuts. But she does
care whether Finn or Alice still
trust her with a knife. Rosemary
stares at herself in a warped
mirror duct taped to the inside
of her closet door for this express
purpose and prays they at least
believe she's sane because she
sure as hell does not.

treasure hunting

She's going to choke herself
one day, searching for a pulse.
There are days when Rosemary
is seized by the need to prove
to herself she's alive. Speaking
isn't enough. Walking about
and making so many people's
lives miserable isn't enough.
Ghosts walk as well – or so says
Janet, and who really knows
whether or not it's safe to trust
Janet? but Rosemary requires
proof all the same and so leaves
thumbprints on wrists and
throat that Finn finds easier to
ignore than fresh scars.

she'd bought him a diamond tie

Rosemary decided to propose
to Finn after a horrible fight
with Alice. She told Janet that
she wanted to never again be
alone but Janet only spat at her
You'll still feel alone I'm sure.
Rosemary ignored her and took
Ivan's silence for approval. She
asked Finn *May I hold your hand
as you're dying* three days later
and he said *No*.

always before the alarm goes off

Rosemary wakes up some mornings
with her throat so dry she can't
breathe without pain. She stumbles
out of bed to choke down a glass of
orange juice – she never drinks
anything but orange juice – and her
eyes are burning the whole while
since she fell asleep in her contacts.
When Rosemary is no longer parched
to the point of muteness, she peels
lenses from irises and – eyes watering
from the sudden contact with the
circulating air – crawls back into bed.
Finn does nothing during this episode
but grunt in his sleep when her icy
feet knock against his legs and she
lets out a first whimper of pain.

everyone has their dreams

It's in moments of clarity and
happiness that Rosemary
realizes how desperately she
wants to die. A calm settles
over her body and mind and
she somehow knows she
could so easily slit her wrists
right then and there if the
opportunity would only arise
and so she can't understand
why no one will just leave her
alone.

44 cents

Finn mailed Rosemary an empty
envelope as an apology, but she
wouldn't be appeased – she knew
it meant his answer hadn't
changed. She kissed twenty-six
year old Brandon in a parking lot
for three hours but he still wouldn't
agree to marry her. She was
forced to go home to find Janet
on the kitchen floor positively
howling with laughter – she'd
somehow found the diamond tie.

a cleaver with a bone handle

Rosemary's third attempt
to catch death unawares
happened on an overcast
June day. She stole the
butcher's largest knife
and hid it in her nightstand.
After Finn finally fell asleep
she took the knife into the
bathroom and tried to cut
her heart from her chest.
She failed but was shocked
into silence for days. When
she finally spoke again, all
she would say was *I couldn't
find it Alice, I honestly
couldn't find it.*

she's lacking in sentiment

Please let me die. Please let me die.
Rosemary once begged her listeners
to give her up and her pleading
was so awfully heartfelt that tears
came to Alice's eyes and Finn
found himself already missing her
desperately – but Janet only scoffed.
She took the phone from Alice's
limp hand and dialed 911.

she swallowed the fork as well

When Alice announced she was engaged
to be married in June, it was only Janet
who got truly upset; Rosemary had
been expecting the news for some weeks
and congratulated her friend as well as
she could but Janet sat seething across
the table. She only calmed down after
eating her glass and deciding she would
marry the next man to walk into the
café. His name was Stuart and he had no
objections to a wedding in May. Janet
thought him divine and knew she'd only
divorce him after seven years of bliss.

the voice of reason

Do you feel unwanted Rosemary?
Janet posed this question as she
rifled through Rosemary's things.
She tucked two or six books into
her purse before ripping a picture
of Rosemary with Alice in half
and throwing Finn's flowers into
the trash. *Because you should.*

not a drop of blood was spilled

She felt herself sinking
one day when she was
supposed to be standing
on her own two feet so
she called out for help
but no one came – Alice
was busy being happy
and Finn was fast asleep –
so Rosemary came up
with her own way to stay
afloat. She unhooked all
the cables from her
television and wrapped
them around both her
neck and the ceiling fan
to try and hoist herself
into the air. For almost
two minutes she felt light
and gloriously in control
but Finn made the
mistake of waking up
and cutting her down
before the lightness
became a permanent
fixture.

he wanted nothing sparkling

Rosemary never gave Finn anything
worth having and he's always resented
her for that. He showered her with
sex and compliments and bits of his
soul but all she wished to give him
in return were sorrows and a gaudy tie
he wouldn't be caught dead in. Out
of spite, he stole her heart but refused
to hold onto anything else. Alice
predicts he'll regret this while Rosemary
is hell bent on making certain Alice
is proven right.

no forecast of rain

Alice grew quiet when she heard
that Rosemary refused to come to
her wedding. Finn quickly gave
her his handkerchief and Janet
even made an actual effort to hide
her glee at the news. Neither
needed to worry though. A full
minute later she began to laugh
and cry at once, so relieved to be
rid of the promise of gloom for
at least one day.

but she's not colorblind

The world has decided it can't forgive
Rosemary for being herself. She's broken
and it doesn't want the responsibility
of piecing her back together so it leaves
her alone to drag her halves into alignment
as best she can and feels at peace with
its decision to give her up to the mercies
of people like Janet who's evil and Alice
who loves Rosemary only when it's
convenient. The world simply can't
forgive her for being sad when colors like
cerulean exist and Rosemary can't bring
herself to care about colors at all – that
splinter of her being was lost when she
was first torn in two at seventeen.

she wore a red dress

Janet was married before Alice
but their weddings were only
two weeks apart. Finn was best
man at both while Rosemary
attended neither. Henri found
her sitting on a park bench one
night cursing her terrible luck.
His sparkling teeth with their
worn silver edges blinded her
and instead of fear she felt relief
when five days later he asked
her to marry him. The wedding
was one week later and it was
only when the last pictures were
taken that Rosemary finally saw
his peg leg and spinning glass eye.

it might even be true

She can be eloquent if she wants to be
but it's not often that Rosemary wishes
to have conversations about why she
is who she is and so no amount of
therapy has done a single thing for her
except made her perfectly convinced
of one awful, defining fact: *some people
were just never meant to be happy.*

she wore the diamond tie

Rosemary picked up her phone
one Saturday evening and instead
of greeting the caller with hello she
said *I've decided to take a break from
the horrors of life and living by dying
Alice dear* and then there was a single
ringing gunshot and the queer
rushing sound of blood. Alice didn't
scream but she wanted to. This is
how what Janet calls *Rosemary's
eighth* happened.

the room is paneled in black and white tile

Rosemary is sitting in front
of the television wondering
why no one has come to find
her. Alice isn't pounding on
the door, Finn isn't calling
every half hour, and even
Ivan is refusing to show his
face. She's lonely. Rosemary
is lonely and all she wants is
to get up and find one of the
few people she loves, but
somehow she can't walk away
from Wheel of Fortune. In her
desperation, she even hopes
Janet might stalk through the
door – but she doesn't. No
one does. No one calls, no
one comes, no one loves her
and so she weeps sitting in front
of Wheel of Fortune. And the
whole while she's sobbing,
feeling alone and unloved, she's
ignorant of why the silence is
really unbroken: Rosemary died
three nights before, and no
one's had the heart to tell her.

Acknowledgments

I would like to thank the editors of *Anomalous Press* where "he had a peg leg too," "the lighter was green," "now maybe you'll understand," "he wasn't trying to lie," and "it was lemonade-colored ash" first appeared.

Thank you to Lisa De Niscia and Whitepoint Press.

I am inestimably grateful to Ken Mikolowski for his wisdom and assistance while putting this collection together.

Many thanks to Keith Taylor for some very necessary guidance early in my poetry career.

And finally, thank you to my family and friends for their support. In particular: my mother, my father, my sisters Namira and Nishat, Andrew Phillips, Asma Khan, Casey Denoyer, Colleen Wagner, Emily Samuelson, Ian McDonald, Jackie Wang, Joshua Lumley, Katy Wagner, Megan Young, Monica Phillips, Najma Khatri, Sahrish Saleem, Sarah Abe, and Samir Islam.

About the Author

Nazifa Islam grew up in Novi, Michigan. She graduated from the University of Michigan with a B.A. in English and is currently pursuing a Master of Fine Arts at Oregon State University. Her poetry and paintings have appeared in a number of publications, including *Anomalous Press*, *From the Depths*, *A Baker's Dozen*, and *Flashquake*. While in London during the summer of 2012, she visited not one but two of Sylvia Plath's houses in Primrose Hill. She can frequently be found banging away at her manual typewriter, regularly updating her blog *Thoughts Interjected*, and dreaming of one day visiting L.M. Montgomery's Prince Edward Island.

Made in the USA
San Bernardino, CA
24 September 2013